Railways & Recollections
The Dartmouth Steam Railway
Mike Heath

© Mike Heath 2021

All rights reserved. No part of this publication may be reproduced, stored in a retrieval system or transmitted, in any form or by any means, electronic, mechanical, photocopying, recording or otherwise, without prior permission in writing from Silver Link Books, Mortons Media Group Ltd..

First published in 2021

British Library Cataloguing in Publication Data

A catalogue record for this book is available from the British Library.

ISBN 978 1 85794 523 2

Silver Link Books
Mortons Media Group Limited
Media Centre
Morton Way
Horncastle
LN9 6JR
Tel/Fax: 01507 529535

email: sohara@mortons.co.uk
Website: https://www.mortonsbooks.co.uk/silverlink

Printed and bound in the Czech Republic

Front cover: **GOODRINGTON SANDS** No 7827 *Lydham Manor* passes Goodrington Sands on 28 May 2016. *Karl Heath*

Title page: **DARTMOUTH** Synchronised steam as the paddle steamer *Kingswear Castle* and GWR 'Manor' Class No 7827 *Lydham Manor* run in parallel as they head for Dartmouth and Kingswear respectively.

Contents

Introduction: a brief history of the branch line to Kingswear	3
The Kingswear branch past and present	4
All change at Kingswear	10
Current locomotives	14
Locomotives formerly used on the line	20
Unusual workings	23
The 'Torbay Express'	24
A journey along the line	29
Heading back to Paignton	60
Index of locations	Inside back cover

Acknowledgements

The author would like to thank the Dartmouth Steam Railway & Riverboat Company for allowing the reproduction of the company's logo, route map and leaflets in this book and David Mitchell for the use of his archive photographs. All photos in the book are by the author unless otherwise credited.

GOODRINGTON
The beach was virtually deserted on the afternoon of 31 August 2015 as No 7827 *Lydham Manor* climbed the steeply graded line away from the station. *Karl Heath*

Introduction

A brief history of the branch line to Kingswear

The need for a rail connection to Dartmouth was clearly evident in the early 19th century. At that time the steep hillsides around the estuary of the River Dart, in South Devon, greatly impaired the transportation of goods to and from the riverside town. Horses laden with pannier baskets provided the only overland transport, and while the development of turnpike roads which allowed access for horse-drawn carriages and carts improved the situation, the transport of goods was still seriously restricted by the severe gradients encountered.

Railways arrived in the area when the South Devon Railway opened its line between Exeter and Plymouth. That was in 1846 when the first section, connecting Exeter with Newton Abbot, was opened. This was extended to Totnes the following year, accompanied by the completion of a branch line to Torquay. The Dartmouth & Torbay Railway Company, which had been set up by local gentlemen, then sought to extend this branch to Dartmouth. Construction of the extension was carried out and opened in stages. Paignton was reached in 1859 and Churston in 1861. The final section to Kingswear following in 1864. Attempts in 1860 to introduce a deviation taking the line to Dittisham Ferry with a view to bridging the Dart at a later date were foiled following objections from an obviously influential local landowner, leaving Dartmouth a ferry ride away from the Kingswear terminus. Nevertheless, a station was provided with full booking and parcels facilities and Dartmouth became unique in possessing a railway station that has never seen a train!

The substantial volume of traffic generated by the Newton Abbot to Kingswear branch in the 1890s substantially helped the development of the Torbay area as a major holiday resort; a situation that continued well into the 1950s. There was also substantial freight traffic; Torquay Gas Works required a steady flow of coal traffic from the quayside at Kingswear, in addition to general merchandise conveyed to local businesses.

In common with many lines at the end of the 1960s, the Paignton to Kingswear branch was under the threat of closure by British Rail. However, the Dart Valley Railway Company, which had already taken over the running of the Totnes to Buckfastleigh branch some years earlier, seized the opportunity to acquire this section of line and almost without a break commenced train services under its own title in 1973. Ownership of the Buckfastleigh branch has since passed to the South Devon Railway Preservation Society, allowing the Dart Valley Railway PLC to acquire boat and bus companies to provide a 'seamless transport of delight through one of the most beautiful areas of England' under the 'Dartmouth Steam Railway & River Boat Company' banner.

The train journey travels through superb scenery. Starting in the traditional seaside town of Paignton, this holiday line then follows the spectacular Torbay coast along the cliffs overlooking the bay before turning inland towards Churston. There then follows a short stretch of pastoral Devon before the line passes along the wooded slopes of the Dart Valley, descending to sea level along the river bank on the final approach to Kingswear. This final stretch is arguably the loveliest section of railway in the country, providing a vista of the Dart estuary and its fascinating variety of boats and yachts with the 'olde world' town of Dartmouth and world-famous Britannia Naval College on the opposite bank.

The Kingswear branch past and present

The archive photographs in this section were taken by David Mitchell in the early 1970s just before ownership of the line passed from British Rail to the Dart Valley Railway Company. They clearly show the run-down state of the railway infrastructure that was taken over by the new company, while the 'present' photographs demonstrate the line's rejuvenation in the ensuing years as part of the development of the Dartmouth Steam Railway & River Boat Company, one of the South West's most popular tourist attractions.

KINGSWEAR In its heyday Kingswear boasted two platform lines with run-round loops, a signal box, turntable, goods shed and yard, quayside sidings, a cattle dock and numerous carriage sidings. The wharf closed in May 1964, with goods traffic ending the following year. The signal box closed on 20 October 1968. By 1971 only the one platform line remained, with the run-round loop retained for engineer's trains. While the goods shed remained, its yard had become a car park. On Saturday 18 September 1971 Class 119 Gloucester RC&W Cross Country DMU (W51067/W59426/W51095) was operating the Kingswear-Paignton shuttles and has just arrived beneath the decaying 'train shed' at Kingswear as the 07.10 service from Paignton. The then closed goods shed is to the left.

The second picture shows the DMU departing shortly afterwards (07.31) with the return service. *Both David Mitchell*

The Dartmouth Steam Railway

KINGSWEAR Forty-six years later the whole scene is much more vibrant. In the intervening years both Kingswear and Dartmouth, across the water, have seen much new development. The old quayside has been rebuilt and extended to cater for the leisure craft moored at the large marina that has been created alongside.

The railway has restored the now rare example of a covered country terminus and the bay platform line has been back in use since 1976. On 6 October 2017 No 7827 *Lydham Manor* has arrived with the first train of the day from Paignton.

Further reading on the Kingswear branch past & present

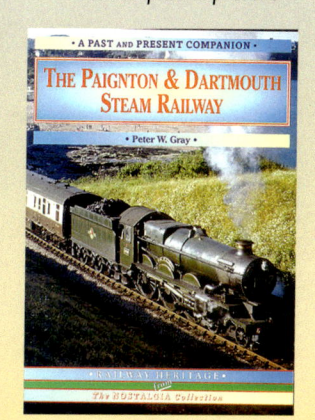

ISBN: 978 1 85895 047 1
published by
Past & Present Books

BRITANNIA HALT Dartmouth has been associated with the Royal Navy for more than 150 years. In 1863 the man o' war HMS *Britannia* was taken out of service and moored off Dartmouth to serve as a training base for Naval Officers. In 1877 the then Prince of Wales was to accompany his two sons to join HMS *Britannia* and for his visit the Great Western Railway constructed a halt alongside the 'higher' steam ferry crossing, the railway's nearest point to the vessel. The platform at 'Kingswear Crossing Halt' (later Britannia Halt) was subsequently retained as an unadvertised stopping place used by both naval cadets and workers from the nearby Philip & Son boatyard. The signal box controlled the crossing gates and approaching signals. In 1971 all railway structures were still in place.

In 1905 HMS *Britannia* was replaced by the impressive Britannia Royal Naval College, built on the hillside overlooking Dartmouth. The unused, derelict halt was removed in 1988. In the 2017 view the crossing gates have been replaced by rise-and-fall barriers and the refurbished signal box now controls all points, signals and crossings on the line. The one exception is the Sands Road crossing in Paignton, which is operated by the locomotive crew.
David Mitchell/Author

The Dartmouth Steam Railway

GREENWAY While the earliest references to 'Greenway' date back to the late 1400s, it is its more recent history that arouses much interest. In 1938 the present Georgian house was bought by Agatha Christie and her husband Max Mallowan and they lived there until their deaths in 1976 and 1978 respectively. In various guises the property and its grounds featured in a number of the author's novels and as such have attracted thousands of visitors since the National Trust, which acquired the estate in 2000, opened it to the public in 2009.

Vehicular access to the house is by pre-arrangement only, so visitors initially arrived by ferry. However, since 2012 they have also been able to travel by steam train and alight at a newly constructed halt just north of the tunnel. In the last days of British Rail ownership a Swindon Class 120 three-car Cross-Country DMU is working the Paignton to Kingswear shuttles on Saturday 21 August 1971; here the 12.47 service from Kingswear emerges from the 495-yard-long Greenway Tunnel.

In the 2017 photograph it is interesting to note that it is the oldest stone-built platelayers' hut that has survived longer than the timber structure standing in the earlier scene. No 7827 *Lydham Manor* has emerged from the tunnel with the first Kingswear departure of the day on 5 October 2017. *David Mitchell/Author*

CHURSTON station once boasted a branch line to Brixham, signal box and cattle dock, in addition to the two passenger platforms and footbridge. Its demise came in the 1960s: the Brixham branch closed in 1963 and the crossing loop and signal box were taken out of use in 1968, leaving a single track to be served by the DMU shuttle services between Paignton and Dartmouth. On Saturday 21 August 1971, with a then rare through working, Class 43 No D855 *Triumph* calls at Churston with 1C36, the 08.45 Kingswear to Cardiff General train. The platform is full of visitors heading home from the Brixham Holiday Camps.

Once having taking over the railway, the Dart Valley Railway Company relaid the branch bay in 1976 and reinstated the loop in 1979 to allow trains to pass each other here once again. It also became apparent that this was the only site where the company could locate workshop buildings for the maintenance and repair of its locomotives and coaches. On 5 October 2017 No 7827 *Lydham Manor* is about to depart with 13.00 Kingswear to Paignton service. *David Mitchell/Author*

The Dartmouth Steam Railway

Right: **GOODRINGTON** On Saturday 21 August 1971, between Goodrington Sands and the Sands Road overbridge, Class 42 No D822 *Hercules* is seen passing Goodrington Sidings with 2B87, the 16.05 Kingswear to Newton Abbot service. Another 'Warship', No 831 *Monarch*, is in the sidings, having arrived with 1B05, the 12.10 Paddington to Paignton train. The carriage holding sidings and adjacent goods shed were constructed in 1930/31 and retained by British Rail when the DVLR leased the line. *David Mitchell*

Below: **GOODRINGTON** On Thursday 5 October *Lydham Manor* is passing the same location where modified sidings, now controlled by Network Rail, remain and a residential development now occupies the site of the goods shed, which closed in 1965. *Author*

All change at Kingswear

As the Great Western Railway developed, so too did the coastal fishing villages and trading ports that it served. Many of these became holiday destinations in their own right and the towns of Kingswear and Dartmouth were no exception. While the increase in road transport brought a decline in passenger numbers and freight trade on the railways in the 1960s, the area's attraction to holidaymakers and travellers continued to grow. This proved a springboard for much development both on the respective hillsides and on the water.

Back in the early 1970s, shortly after the Dart Valley Railway Company had started to revive the Paignton to Dartmouth line to continue the GWR tradition of playing a major part in South Devon's tourism market, the Darthaven Marina was founded at Kingswear and commenced developing facilities for waterborne visitors.

For more than 40 years I have visited Dartmouth many times and recorded, through photography, the rapid development of the area and in particular the railway. Presented here are photographs taken in the 1970s and 1980s alongside present-day views from the same vantage points.

KINGSWEAR In July 1977 Kingswear station was still in 'as taken over' condition with the goods shed and awning still in place.

The oldest ferry with a continuous service at Kingswear is the 'historic' Lower Ferry seen here. When the railway arrived in 1865 the Dartmouth & Torbay Railway bought the ferry operation and leased it to a local postmaster, Tom Avis. When the Great Western Railway took control it found that its own passenger ferry was suffering due to the popularity of the Lower Ferry service. Eventually the rights to the Lower Ferry crossing were passed to the Borough Council to avoid further problems. The lease was taken up by a Mr Peters and the service was saved. In 1929 new, more powerful tugs were brought in and they have remained virtually unchanged in basic design since then. However, the float's ramps are now hydraulically operated in lieu of the chains seen in this view.

In the August 2013 image the paddle steamer *Kingswear Castle*, which in 2012 returned to its home waters of the River Dart after an absence of 47 years, is passing a colourful and more densely populated town. The station is more clearly visible, as is the railway company's 'signal box' offices.

KINGSWEAR In July 1985 No 7827 *Lydham Manor* awaits departure time. One of the earliest of many major improvements made at Kingswear was the restoration of the bay platform line seen in the foreground.

The railway bisected the land that was bought for the Darthaven Marina development and the owners had to invest a considerable sum in the construction of the crossing that is clearly visible in the October 2017 photograph at the far end of the extended wharf. Note the increase in the number and concentration of boats in the estuary in the present-day view. The same locomotive, *Lydham Manor*, now in British Railways lined black livery, is receiving attention from the footplate crew before returning to Paignton.

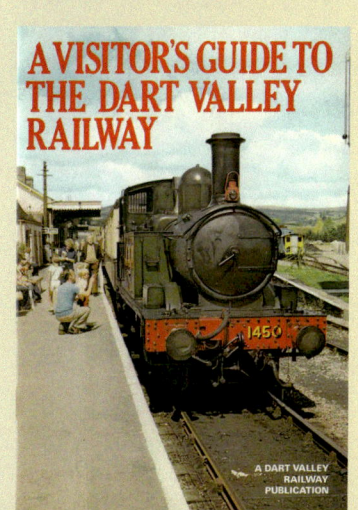

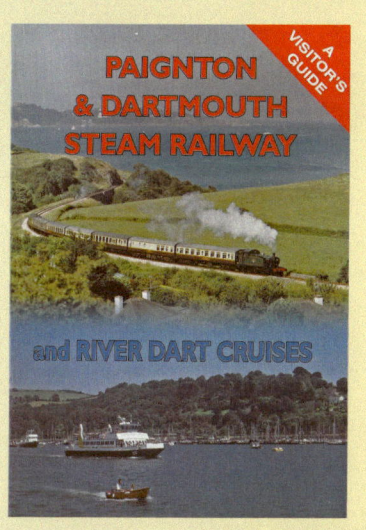

KINGSWEAR Between Greenway and Kingswear, when first constructed, the railway crossed three creeks on low timber viaducts. Those at Longwood and Noss were demolished after the line was moved inland around the creeks on 20 May 1923, and Hoodown Viaduct, just outside the station, was replaced in 1928 by the double-track steel structure seen here. This, together with the provision of a larger turntable, allowed the GWR to operate larger locomotives to Kingswear. In the July 1988 view No 5239 *Goliath* has crossed the viaduct and is heading for Paignton.

Twenty-eight years later on 2 June 2016 GWR '4500' Class 2-6-2T No 5542 arrives at the terminus with an afternoon train. No 5542 spent the summer of that year working services on the South Devon line.

KINGSWEAR The failure of plans to build a bridge across the Dart between Greenway and Dittisham brought about the development of the Dartmouth Floating Bridge (Higher Ferry), which first opened in 1829. Early examples were driven by horse power, with horses working a treadmill drawing the floating bridge across on chains. Despite earlier attempts to introduce steam power, it was 1867 before the poor horses were permanently replaced. Following a number of changes in ownership, Philip & Son took charge in 1918 and built a new ferry that was propelled across the river by paddle wheels running on wire ropes. The use of wire ropes continues to this day. The ferry in the 1977 photograph dates from 1960 and had a diesel-electric motor to power the paddles. It was named *Philip* and was able to carry 15 cars. (Note that the railway 'Halt' by the crossing on the opposite bank is still standing).

On 15 July 2009 the 'new' Dartmouth Higher Ferry was introduced, seen here in 2015. This vessel had virtually twice the capacity of *Philip* and allowed simultaneous loading and disembarking of vehicles, making the crossing quicker and more efficient.

Current locomotives (June 2021)

GOODRINGTON SANDS No 4555 passes Goodrington Sands on the way back to Paignton in August 2001, by which time it had acquired the name *Warrior*.

GWR '4500' Class 2-6-2T No 4555 (*Warrior*)

The '4500' Class was first introduced in 1906 and was to become the mainstay of many Great Western and British Railways Western Region services in Devon and Cornwall.

Built by the GWR in Swindon in 1924, No 4555 worked occasionally on the Buckfastleigh branch and headed the last BR freight train on that line in 1962. It was purchased for preservation straight from BR service in 1965 and was the first engine to arrive on the newly preserved Buckfastleigh line. When ownership of the Paignton to Dartmouth line changed in 1973, No 4555 was one of the locomotives transferred over to work what was then known as the Torbay Steam Railway. No 4555 was withdrawn from service in 2007 and its overhaul, which started in 2014, was completed in 2020. Since then an arrangement between the Dartmouth Steam Railway and the East Somerset Railway will see 4555 based in Somerset for 3 years.

KINGSWEAR No 4555 stands at Kingswear station on 21 July 1992.

The Dartmouth Steam Railway

GWR 'Manor' Class 4-6-0 No 7827 *Lydham Manor*
No 7827 is an example of the later batch of the class and, though unmistakably a GWR 4-6-0, it is actually a British Railways locomotive. Built in 1950 at the Great Western Railway's Swindon Works, No 7827 was allocated to Chester but later spent time at Oswestry and Shrewsbury before it was withdrawn in October 1965. Acquired by Woodhams' scrapyard in May 1966 it became the fifth locomotive to be rescued from there, in June 1970, and was restored at Buckfastleigh by the Dart Valley Railway in 1973. It then moved to the then new Torbay Steam Railway, where it has remained ever since.

Right: **KINGSWEAR** For most of its preservation life *Lydham Manor* has carried the railway's Great Western green livery, as seen in this photo of the loco arriving at Kingswear.

Below: **BRITANNIA CROSSING** In 2011 No 7827 was reintroduced at the Churston Heritage Festival carrying British Railways all-black livery and bearing the temporary number and nameplates of No 7800 *Torquay Manor* for the festival. In this guise it was photographed approaching Britannia Crossing with the last train of the day on 30 May 2011.

GWR '5205' Class 2-8-0 tank No 5239 (*Goliath*)
This class was introduced by Churchward in 1910 for heavy freight work in the Welsh Valleys, where No 5239 worked on coal traffic from 1924, the year it emerged from Swindon Works, until the demise of steam in 1963. It was transferred to Woodham's scrapyard in Barry and languished there until 1973 when it was rescued by the Dart Valley Railway. It arrived at Newton Abbot in June 1973, where most of the restoration work was carried out. In June 1976 it was transferred to Paignton for completion, entering traffic, with the name *Goliath*, in 1978. 5239 was taken out of service on the Dartmouth Steam Railway at the end of the 2015 season and stored at Churston works. In October 2017 the locomotive was transferred to the East Somerset Railway for a contract overhaul and returned to the South Devon line in April 2020.

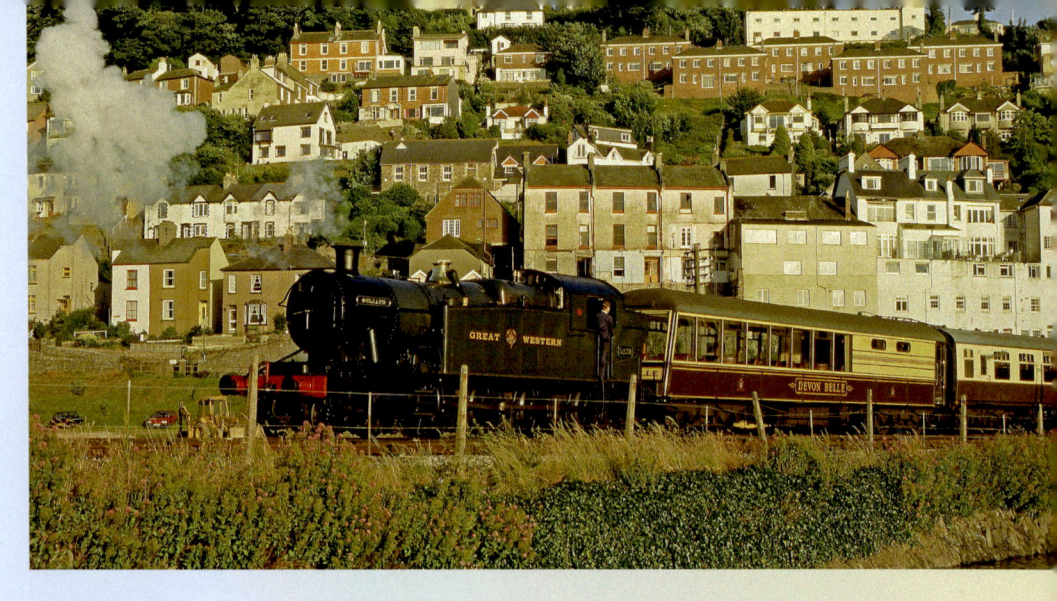

Above: **KINGSWEAR** On the evening of 1 July 1988 *Goliath* is shunting coaches at Kingswear for an evening 'Special'.

Left: **KINGSWEAR** Twenty-one years later No 5239 arrives at Kingswear on 25 July 2009.

The Dartmouth Steam Railway

British Railways Standard 4MT 4-6-0 No 75014 (*Braveheart*)

No 75014 was built in December 1951 at Swindon and is one of the British Railways Standard Class 4 4-6-0s that was designed for use on the Western, London Midland and Southern regions of the recently nationalised rail network. Its short life was spent working around the London Midland Region until it was withdrawn from Shrewsbury shed in December 1966. For 14 years it rotted in Barry scrapyard and donated parts to other locomotives until it was purchased as a wreck in 1981. A group based on the North Yorkshire Moors Railway brought it back to steam in 1994. From 1995 to 1998 it was the mainstay of the 'Jacobite' tourist train from Fort William to Mallaig. It returned to Scotland in 2000 and was named *Braveheart* in recognition of the Mel Gibson film, which was shot in the West Highlands. In 2002 it was bought by the Dartmouth Steam Railway & River Boat Company, but only worked for just two years as its boiler certificate expired in 2004. *Braveheart* subsequently received a major overhaul that took many years, eventually seeing a return to service in December 2016.

Above: **MOORGATES (NYMR)**
No 75014 passes Moorgates on the North Yorkshire Moors Railway on 6 October 2001.

Left: **GOODRINGTON SANDS**
Three years later, in September 2004, it was photographed climbing past a strangely vacant Goodrington Sands.

GWR '4200' Class 2-8-0 tank No 4277 (*Hercules*)

Another GWR 2-8-0 heavy freight tank, built at Swindon in 1920, like loco No 5239 it spent its entire working life hauling coal trains in the South Wales Valleys, then languished in Woodham's scrapyard on Barry Island for more than 20 years until privately purchased in 1986. Restoration was followed by visits to a number of preserved railways up and down the country before it was purchased by the Dartmouth Steam Railway in 2008. For the last few months of its boiler certificate, before withdrawn for overhaul, it visited the Churnet Valley Railway at Cheddleton, where it was painted in British Railways black livery and temporarily lost it nameplates. This was the first time a locomotive owned by the DSR had gone on medium- or long-term loan to another railway; prior to this, only 'Manor' No 7827 *Lydham Manor* had made guest appearances elsewhere, and then only for gala weekends. 4277's boiler certificate expired in February 2018 and the locomotive is currently under overhaul..

Above: **KINGSWEAR** No 4277 runs round its train at Kingswear on 28 July 2008.

Below: **CHURNET VALLEY RAILWAY** On 29 October 2017, in BR black livery, the engine is seen again on the Churnet Valley Railway.

Above: **ESK VALLEY (NYMR)** On completion of its overhaul in 2019 No 2253 underwent trials on the North Yorkshire Moors Railway before moving to the Dartmouth Steam Railway. It was photographed passing Esk Valley cottages with a demonstration freight working on 28 September 2019. The locomotive was outshopped in a plum coloured livery, inspired by the Canadian Pacific Railway and was named *Omaha* in honour of owner Peter Best's father's involvement with the D-Day landings at Omaha beach. It arrived in South Devon in 2020.

Ex-USA 'S160' Class 2-8-0 No 2253

To help plug a gap in its operating fleet following the withdrawal of its two heavy freight tank locomotives *Goliath* and *Hercules*, the railway agreed a ten-year loan agreement for 'S160' Class 2-8-0 No 2253 to run on the Dartmouth Steam Railway on completion of its overhaul.

The United States Army Transportation Corps 'S160' was a class of 2-8-0 steam locomotives designed for use on heavy freight work in Europe during the Second World War. A total of 2,120 were built and they worked on railroads across the world. Although the American machine may seem somewhat unusual in the fleet of former Great Western Railway steam locomotives usually associated with this preserved railway, the type nevertheless has a historical connection with the area. During the Second World War they were used to support the D-Day invasion force prior to embarkation for Normandy, including the contingent that sailed from Dartmouth.

No 2253, built in 1943, was previously based on the North Yorkshire Moors Railway.

Above: **GROSMONT (NYMR)**
Seen in the yard at Grosmont on 17 May 2014, 'S160' No 2253 had been cosmetically restored to go on loan to Locomotion, Shildon. *Courtesy of Kenneth Snowdon*

Left: **MOORGATES (NYMR)**
No 2253 powers through Moorgates on the North Yorkshire Moors Railway on a cold winter's day back in the 1990s. *Courtesy of E. Fisher*

Locomotives formerly used on the line

GWR '4575' Class 2-6-2T No 4588 (*Trojan*)

The '4500' design was later modified to create the '4575' Class, larger side tanks being the main difference. One example is No 4588, which was one of the locomotives rescued from Barry scrapyard when it was purchased by the Dart Valley Railway Association in 1971. It returned to service the following year. With No 4555 it was transferred to work on the Kingswear branch, where it was given the name *Trojan*. Deemed surplus to requirements, it was sold in 2015 after being out of service for more than a decade.

Right: **KINGSWEAR** No 4588 runs round its train at Kingswear in June 1977.

Below: **WATERSIDE** No 4588 is working hard climbing away from Waterside on 27 July 1999, by which time it had received its nameplates.

The Dartmouth Steam Railway

GWR '64xx' Class 0-6-0PT No 6435

No 6435, another product of the Swindon factory, dates from 1934 and was one of the 40-strong '64xx' Class of Great Western Railway pannier tanks that operated all over the GWR system. Most of its working life was spent on passenger duties in South Wales, but it ended its days working out of Yeovil. No 6435 was purchased directly from British Rail by the Dart Valley Railway, the then operators of today's South Devon Railway, and arrived at Buckfastleigh in October 1965. It was used regularly during the SDR's early days of preservation, then in the 1970s, like other locomotives, it was transferred to the company's Paignton to Kingswear line. In 2008 No 6435 was declared too small for this heavily graded line and was sold for use on the Bodmin & Wenford Railway in Cornwall.

KINGSWEAR No 6435 departs from Kingswear on 25 July 1992.

GWR 'Hall' Class 4-6-0 No 4920 *Dumbleton Hall*

On 21 November 1999 No 4920 *Dumbleton Hall* was in steam at Buckfastleigh for the last time before the expiry of its 10-year boiler certificate. It is a Collett-designed GWR '4900' Class locomotive built in Swindon in March 1929, and most of its working life was spent in the West Country. It finished its active British Railways service at Oxford in December 1965, becoming the longest-serving member of the class and outliving most of its classmates on the main line by at least two years. It is also the oldest 'Hall' Class locomotive to survive in preservation. In 1976 it was bought from Woodhams' scrapyard in Barry by the Dumbleton Hall Preservation Society and rebuilt at Buckfastleigh, being fully restored in 1988. It then worked on a number of preserved lines before the expiry of its boiler certificate in November 1999. Since then it has languished at Buckfastleigh awaiting overhaul. In December 2020 the South Devon Railway Trust and Dumbleton Hall Preservation Society announced an agreement to sell the locomotive to a third-party and the loco has since been moved to a new undisclosed home.

Above and right: **KINGSWEAR** On 19 July 1992 *Dumbleton Hall* was in action on the Paignton to Kingswear line.

Unusual workings

Above: Over the May Bank Holiday weekend in 2011 the railway held a 'Heritage Festival', and one of the highlights of this event was the debut of No 7827 *Lydham Manor* in fully lined BR black livery, running as No 7800 *Torquay Manor* for the weekend. At Churston there was a huge military encampment on the school grounds adjacent to the railway, right down to the workshop. An intense timetable was in operation over the weekend, with Nos 4277, 5239 and 7827 all working trains, which included a freight train and a war ('troop') train running up and down with a mixed rake of coaches and transport-carrying freight wagons.

Right: **WATERSIDE** 2014 marked the 150th anniversary of the opening of the Paignton-Kingswear section of the line, and the railway marked the anniversary with a series of events including a special gala over the third weekend of August. The whole of the line's operational fleet was in action, working an intensive timetable of passenger services, demonstration ballast trains and even a two-coach shuttle operated by the line's two diesel shunters. On the lovely morning of 16 August 2014 No 4277 is captured passing Waterside with the demonstration ballast train. *Karl Heath*

The 'Torbay Express'

GOODRINGTON SANDS In the halcyon days of the Great Western Railway, steam locomotives hauled the company's 'Torbay Express' from London's Paddington station to Torquay and Paignton. Nowadays on selected summer Sundays a steam-hauled rail tour under the 'Torbay Express' banner recreates that bygone era, when steam trains carried holidaymakers to their summer holidays on the 'English Riviera'. Running from Bristol Temple Meads station, the steam-hauled train follows the route of Brunel's picturesque line, racing across the Somerset levels before passing along the beautiful Devon coastline to Kingswear, on what is proclaimed to be one of the most enchanting railway journeys in the world. Over the years these trains have been hauled by a variety of steam locomotives. On 18 August 2013 former Southern Region 'West Country' Class 4-6-2 No 34046 *Braunton* was on duty and is seen passing Goodrington Sands en route to Kingswear.

The Dartmouth Steam Railway

KINGSWEAR Later that day the sun shone for the travellers to sample the delights of Dartmouth, and remained out for the return journey in the late afternoon.

Railways & Recollections

Above and left: **KINGSWEAR** Back on 27 July 2008 Great Western Railway 'King' Class 4-6-0 No 6024 *King Edward I* travelled down from Bristol at the head of the 'Torbay Express', and for the Paignton to Kingswear leg carried a special 'Thank You Barry' headboard in recognition of the service of Barry Cogar, who had recently resigned after being the railway's General Manager since 1972. The 'King' made a splendid GWR image hauling suitably liveried coaches along the river bank on the return trip.

BRITANNIA CROSSING This panoramic view, from 17 August 2014, shows *Braunton* with the return leg of the 'Torbay Express' climbing away from Britannia Crossing. *Karl Heath*

ROUTE MAP

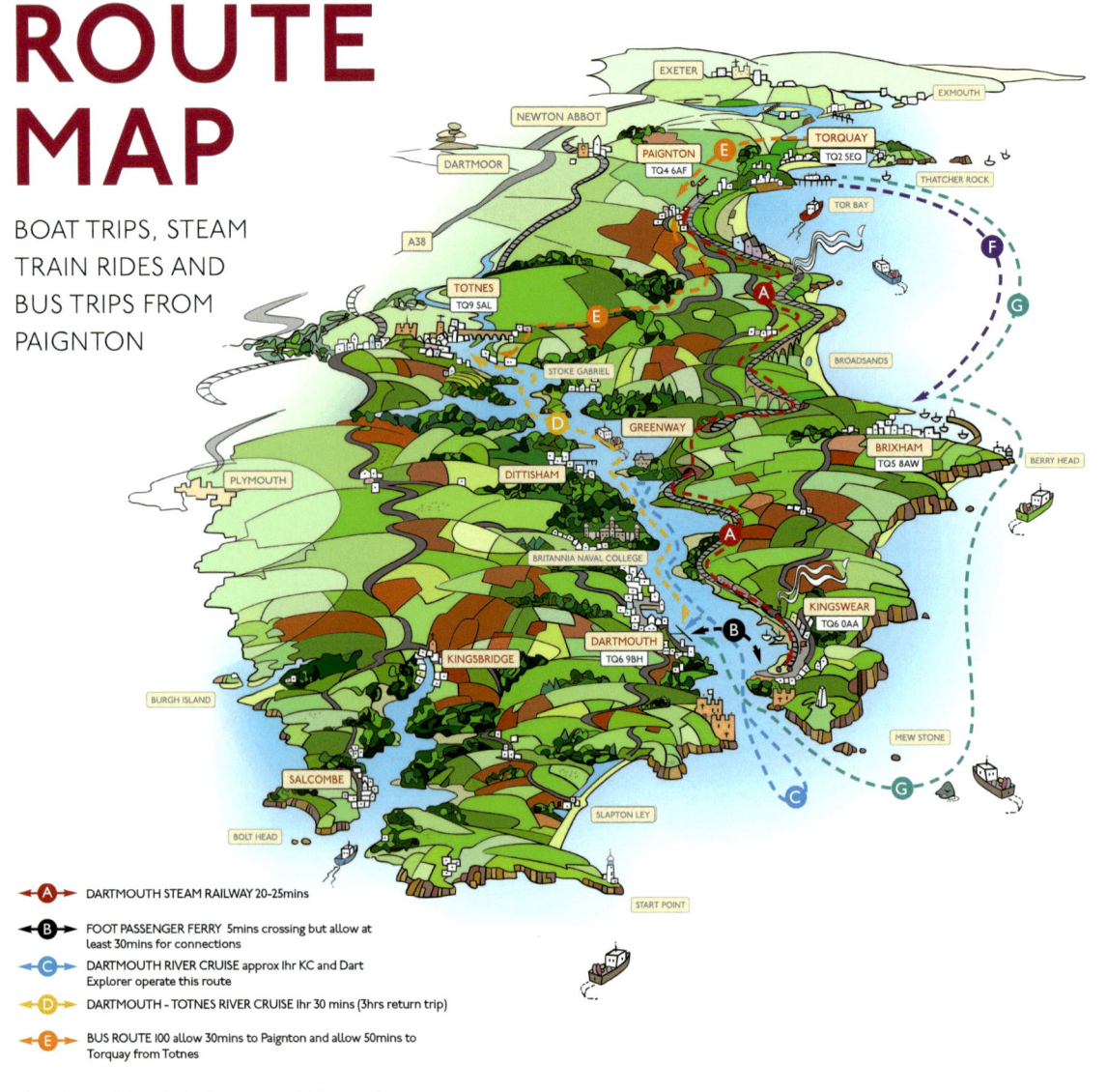

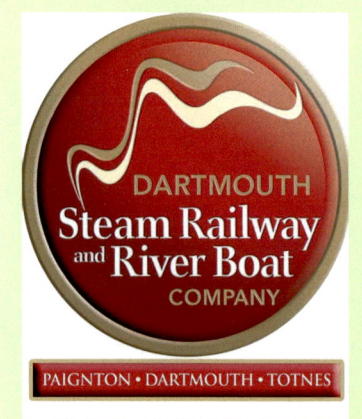

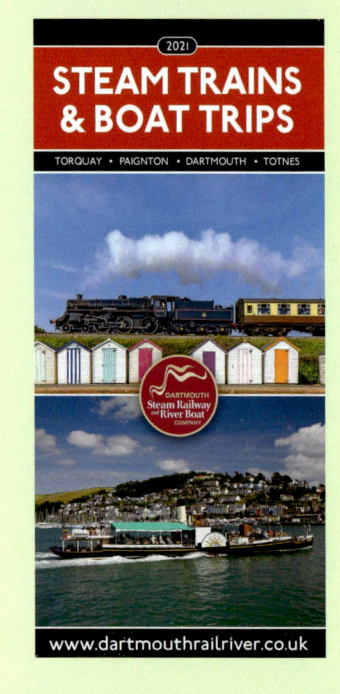

BOAT TRIPS, STEAM TRAIN RIDES AND BUS TRIPS FROM PAIGNTON

- **A** — DARTMOUTH STEAM RAILWAY 20-25mins
- **B** — FOOT PASSENGER FERRY 5mins crossing but allow at least 30mins for connections
- **C** — DARTMOUTH RIVER CRUISE approx 1hr KC and Dart Explorer operate this route
- **D** — DARTMOUTH - TOTNES RIVER CRUISE 1hr 30 mins (3hrs return trip)
- **E** — BUS ROUTE 100 allow 30mins to Paignton and allow 50mins to Torquay from Totnes

Please refer to the Western Lady website at westernladyferry.com for:

- **F** — BRIXHAM - TORQUAY FERRY 30mins. The Western Lady Service operates on this route
- **G** — TORQUAY - BRIXHAM - DARTMOUTH SEA VOYAGE. As a stand alone trip or part of a combined ticket - ask for details

DARTMOUTH Steam Railway and River Boat COMPANY

PAIGNTON · DARTMOUTH · TOTNES

2021 STEAM TRAINS & BOAT TRIPS

TORQUAY · PAIGNTON · DARTMOUTH · TOTNES

www.dartmouthrailriver.co.uk

A journey along the line

PAIGNTON

PAIGNTON On the platform a signal diagram board is located above the station sign on the wall, enabling passengers to follow the progress of the train. The illuminated lights at Churston show the location of the train on its way to Kingswear.

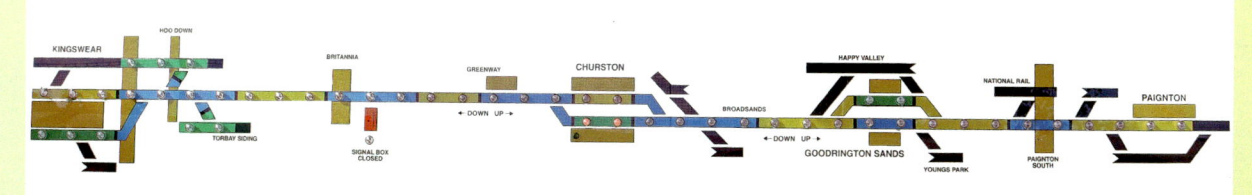

PAIGNTON The Dartmouth Steam Railway's station at Paignton is adjacent to the town's main railway station. When the company took over the line it purchased the five 'Park Sidings' from British Rail and retained the two easternmost ones as a platform and loop line. On the others they built passenger facilities, offices and a locomotive shed at the southern end. The original station building (seen in the first picture) was rebuilt in a more traditional GWR style and opened in 2012, with new offices for the railway and boats having been opened at Kingswear a year earlier.

GOODRINGTON SANDS On leaving Paignton the train passes over the Sands Road crossing and alongside the Network Rail sidings (see page 9) before emerging alongside Goodrington Sands. The station here opened as Goodrington Halt on 9 July 1928, the word 'Sands' being added two months later; in May 1969 the term 'Halt' was removed. On a beautiful summer morning in July 2008 No 4277 *Hercules* has just started away from the station with the first train of the day.

The Dartmouth Steam Railway

GOODRINGTON SANDS With its gently shelving sandy beaches, clean and calm water with a Quality Coast Award, the highly accessible Goodrington Sands is a major attraction on the aptly named 'English Riviera'. Overlooking the beach are the gigantic flumes of Splashdown Quaywest, the largest outdoor water park in the United Kingdom, which opened as Quaywest Water Park in 1988. On 18 August 2013 early-morning beachcombers are treated to the sight of No 7827 *Lydham Manor* working its way to Kingswear.

Right: **GOODRINGTON SANDS** For the summer of 2018 the railway hired the Great Western Railway London Transport liveried pannier tank No L94. Its usual base is the Tyseley Locomotive Works in Birmingham. *Karl Heath*

Below: **GOODRINGTON SANDS** The iconic British seaside beach hut is well represented at Goodrington as No 7820 *Dinmore Manor*, on loan from Dinmore Manor Locomotive Ltd, works tender-first on 3 October 2015. *Karl Heath*

The Dartmouth Steam Railway

33

Below: **GOODRINGTON SANDS** The coastal footpath that runs alongside the railway at this point gives a panoramic view over the beach, a perfect location for photographing late-afternoon trains. In 2016 GWR '4575' Class 2-6-2T 'Small Prairie' No 5542, built in 1928, spent the summer working services on the line and is seen here on 2 June 2016.

Right: **GOODRINGTON SANDS** A second 2018 visitor taking up a summer residency in South Devon was the Didcot based BR blue-liveried GWR 'King' Class No 6023 *King Edward II*. On 13 July 2018 the 'King' climbs away from the station. *Karl Heath*

Below and right: **WATERSIDE** The climb to the summit at Churston continues as the golden sands of Goodrington give way to rocky cliffs and small coves at Waterside. On 31 May 2011 No 4277 *Hercules* clings to the ledge above Saltern Cove before passing beneath Sugar Loaf Hill.

Right: **SUGAR LOAF HILL** The sea view from the footpath on Sugar Loaf Hill covers a wide expanse of Torbay including Brixham in the distance. No 75014 *Braveheart* drifts down towards Paignton on 11 June 2018.

Below: **SUGAR LOAF HILL** Other than the growth of the vegetation, little has changed on 8 June 2012 as visiting GWR '4900' Class No 4936 *Kinlet Hall* passes.

Left: **SUGAR LOAF HILL** sweeps down into a narrow valley where Waterside Holiday Park is situated. On 28 July 2008 No 7827 *Lydham Manor*, in GWR green livery, approaches the narrow bridge over the footpath that gives the holiday park access to the sea. *Author*

Below: **SUGAR LOAF HILL** *King Edward II* passes over the footpath with an afternoon service on 14 July 2018. *Karl Heath*

SUGAR LOAF HILL Double-headed trains are unusual on the Dartmouth Steam Railway, but on 8 June 2012 the pairing of No 7827 *Lydham Manor*, now carrying British Railways lined black livery and visiting No 4936 *Kinlet Hall* made a fine spectacle as they passed the caravan park in a brief shaft of sunlight.

Left: **BROADSANDS VIADUCT** As the line continues to climb, the first of the three viaducts along the route is crossed. Broadsands Viaduct is 51 yards long, 75 feet high and has four arches. No 5239 *Goliath* crosses on 26 July 2000.

Below left: **BROADSANDS VIADUCT** In this view of the viaduct from across the bay at Broadsands, No 4277 *Hercules* heads a train on 16 August 2014. *Karl Heath*

Below: **BROADSANDS VIADUCT** No 75014 *Braveheart* has just passed over the viaduct in this view from the main A279 Paignton to Brixham road on 2 September 2004.

The Dartmouth Steam Railway

HOOKHILLS VIADUCT The railway then passes through a deep cutting before again coming within sight of the beach as it crosses the longer Hookhills Viaduct. This has nine arches, is 116 yards long and stands 85 feet above a residential estate in the valley below. No 4277 *Hercules* is seen crossing on 16 August 2014 and 2 June 2016. *Karl Heath/Author*

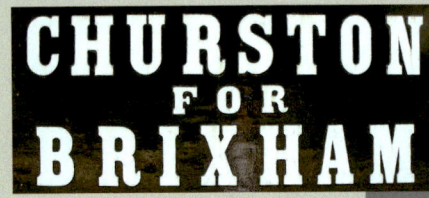

CHURSTON When the Dart Valley Light Railway plc took control of the line on 30 December 1972, Churston became an important centre for engineering on the railway. The signal box was reopened in 1979 and the following year the former Brixham bay platform was relaid. In 1981 the turntable, formerly at Goodrington, was installed alongside the Brixham junction just out of shot on the other side of the road bridge in this photo. When control of the signalling for the line was transferred to Britannia Crossing at Kingswear in 1991 the signal box was closed. A locomotive workshop was built behind the up (towards Paignton) platform in 1993 and the station building restored and reopened. The Brixham bay platform was then covered by a carriage workshop in 1996. On 25 July 2009 No 5239 *Goliath* draws into the station.

The Dartmouth Steam Railway

41

CHURSTON opened as BRIXHAM ROAD 14th MARCH 1861

CHURSTON The passing loop allows two trains to operate on the line in high season. On a glorious September 2004 afternoon a Kingswear-bound train, in the hands of No 75014 *Braveheart*, eases to a stop.

GREENWAY HALT From Churston to Kingswear the journey is virtually all downhill, initially through rolling countryside. On 9 October 2017 the 'Manor', facing Paignton, departs from Greenway Halt.

The Dartmouth Steam Railway

43

GREENWAY HALT Travellers interested in visiting Greenway House and Garden can now arrive by steam train (and shuttle bus for those who prefer not to walk) by boarding at Paignton or Kingswear and catching the bus connection at Churston or at this halt. Those walking from the halt are treated to a beautiful 30-minute woodland path from the station platform which takes them straight to the House and Garden. The station was constructed by the northern portal of the 495-yard-long Greenway Tunnel.

GREENWAY HOUSE AND GARDEN is run by the National Trust and nestles on the banks of the beautiful River Dart, boasting simply stunning views. Formerly the holiday home of Agatha Christie and her family, it holds the family collection of the famous author and the gardens play host to more that 2,700 species of trees and woody plants. It is well worth a visit.

The Dartmouth Steam Railway

GREENWAY VIADUCT Just south of the tunnel is the listed Greenway Viaduct, the third on the line. Much more hidden from view than the others, it has ten arches, is 495 yards long and bridges a steep wooded valley on the east side of the River Dart. In both these photographs the train is climbing towards the tunnel.

NOSS CREEK

Heading down through the woods towards Kingswear the railway curves around Noss Creek. This inlet has a rich history of shipbuilding that dates back to the 1880s, when Simpson Strickland & Company Limited first built a shipyard here. In 1917 the yard was purchased by Philip & Son, which for almost a century and a half provided employment for hundreds of local men and turned out thousands of tonnes of historic naval vessels, lightships for Trinity House and even Chay Blyth's *British Steel* round-the-world yacht.

The Second World War saw the shipyard build more than 200 vessels as part of the war effort, and despite losing 20 men, who were killed by Luftwaffe bombs in September 1942, the shipyard survived and continued to operate until the demise of the British shipbuilding industry eventually caused it to close its doors in 1999. In March 2016 Premier Marinas bought the site with the aim of transforming it into 'the UK's finest marina, with a vibrant commercial community that will sensitively work alongside the natural beauty of the site to secure the future of the marina for boaters and bring visitors, employment and investment opportunities into the area.' In June 2017 the company submitted its plans to regenerate the 37-acre site.

When the railway was first constructed the two inlets (left and right of the shipyard in the photo) at Noss Creek were spanned by two viaducts until the 'inland' route around the back of the creek was completed in 1923. On 17 August 2014 *Braunton* passes the creek with the return leg of the 'Torbay Express'. *Karl Heath*

The Dartmouth Steam Railway

47

LONG WOOD Between Noss Creek and Britannia Crossing the railway cuts a path through Long Wood. This is ancient woodland, largely owned by the National Trust, with semi-natural oak stretching over 100 acres. It is a haven for wildlife and in late November the colours are fantastic. For the ornithologists the wood is inhabited by blue tits, marsh tits, woodpeckers, buzzards, tawny owls, sparrowhawks and jays. Climbing towards the bridge that carries the road down to Noss Marina on 5 October 2017 is No 7827 *Lydham Manor*.

Top left: **BRITANNIA CROSSING** L94 emerges from the woods on 12 June 2018, giving its train's passengers the first glimpse of what will become a gradually expanding vista of Dartmouth Harbour.

Bottom left: **BRITANNIA CROSSING** A few years earlier, in its pseudo Great Western Railway livery, the 'Manor' cruises past Britannia Crossing and the signal box *(above)* that now controls signalling and points along the whole line from the wall-mounted control panel seen below.

The Dartmouth Steam Railway

BRITANNIA CROSSING No 4277 *Hercules* pulls away from the crossing on a deceptively windy 2 November 2015. The strength of the wind has caused the temporary suspension of Higher Ferry services, and the ferry is being held in mid-river until the winds ease.

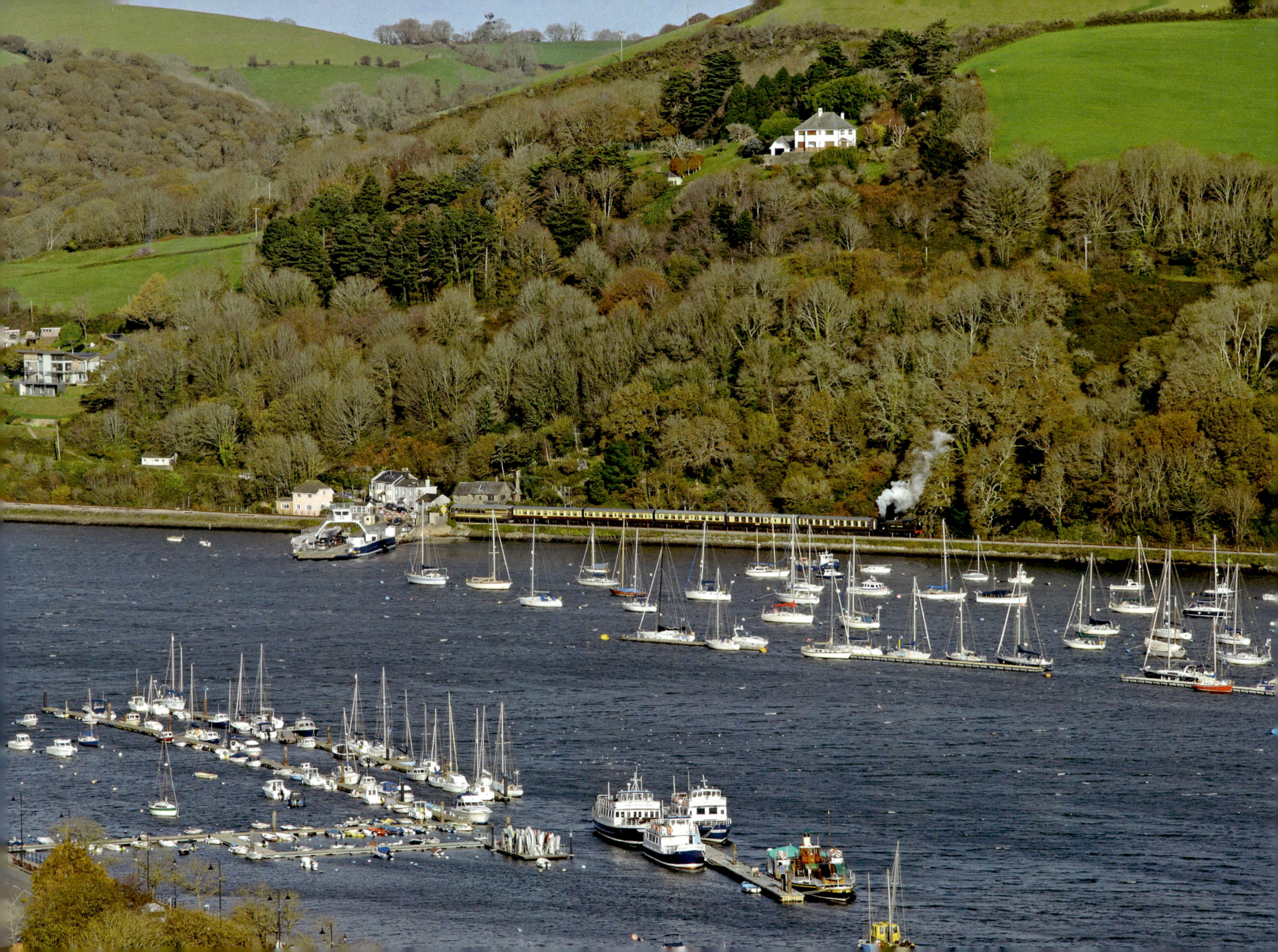

The Dartmouth Steam Railway

51

Left and above: **BRITANNIA CROSSING** Jawbones Hill, above Dartmouth, gives a wonderful panoramic view over the town, river, railway and out to sea. From here you can track the progress of a train as it makes its way to the Kingswear terminus.

KINGSWEAR Along this section of line there is a footpath that runs between the railway and the water's edge, which gives superb close-up views of the railway and estuary as well as a splendid panorama of the Dartmouth waterfront opposite and the Britannia Royal Naval College high on the hill above the town.

The Dartmouth Steam Railway

Right: **KINGSWEAR** Before entering the station the train passes across Hoodown Viaduct over the entrance to Waterhead Creek. The white property at the head of the creek is a former tidal corn mill. The 'wear' in Kingswear actually refers to this tidal mill, which used weirs to control the water in and out, allowing more regular power for its corn grinding in Waterhead Creek. ('King' derives from Kingston, a village on the plateau above Kingswear.)

Below: **KINGSWEAR** The Royal Britannia Naval College dominates the background in this 28 July 2008 photograph of No 4277 *Hercules* arriving at the terminus with a morning train.

KINGSWEAR station has level access to the street and is adjacent to the former Yacht Club Hotel, the pontoon for the Dartmouth Passenger Ferry and the slipway of the Dartmouth Lower Ferry (bottom right). The Yacht Club Hotel at the southern end of the station, which has recently been redeveloped into luxury flats, was opened by the original railway company in 1866, primarily for passengers on the ocean-going ships that called at Dartmouth at that time.

The Dartmouth Steam Railway

KINGSWEAR station comprises a very rare wooden 100-foot-long train shed with a more conventional canopy extending along the platform. Passengers will note that the train stops further along the platform to allow the locomotive to run round using the crossover at this end of the platform track. The bay platform does not have a locomotive release road, so is only used for occasional departures such as the 'Torbay Express'.

A car park and boat storage area now occupies the former goods yard between the station and the waterfront. There is a long footbridge at the north end of the station; this is not connected to the platforms, but carries a footpath from the main road across to the waterfront, where it gives access to the path along the railway to Britannia Crossing. Another car park at the north end of the station is on the site of the turntable and carriage sidings.

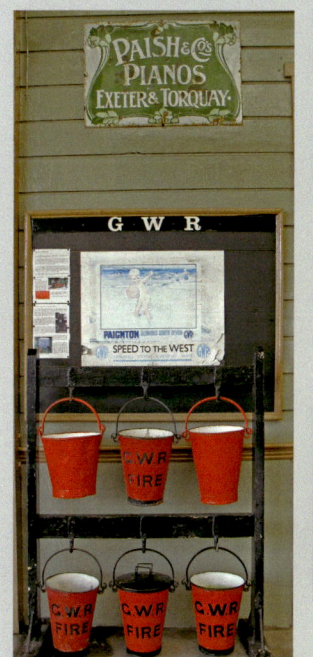

KINGSWEAR This signal-box-style building was completed in 2011 to house the offices for the railway and boats company.

KINGSWEAR For visitors arriving at Kingswear the choices are multiple. The Dartmouth Steam Railway & Riverboat Company runs excursions and cruises to suit all. The circular 'Round Robin' includes a tourist bus ride, a steam train journey and a river boat cruise calling in at the quaint towns of Paignton, Dartmouth and Totnes on the way.

Those staying around Dartmouth can take in a wonderful circular boat trip affording views of Bayard's Cove, Kingswear and Dartmouth castles, the Britannia Royal Naval College, Dittisham village, Sir Walter Raleigh's boathouse, Greenway Quay and the estate of the late Dame Agatha Christie.

A favourite excursion involves a 9-mile sail along nearly all of the navigable part of the beautiful River Dart between the delightful and unique towns of Dartmouth and Totnes. En route passengers can view the magnificent buildings of the Britannia Royal Naval College, Agatha Christie's Greenway estate, the riverside villages of Stoke Gabriel and Dittisham, the Sharpham estate with its vineyards, and the steeply wooded hillsides plunging down to the water's edge, providing unparalleled scenic views.

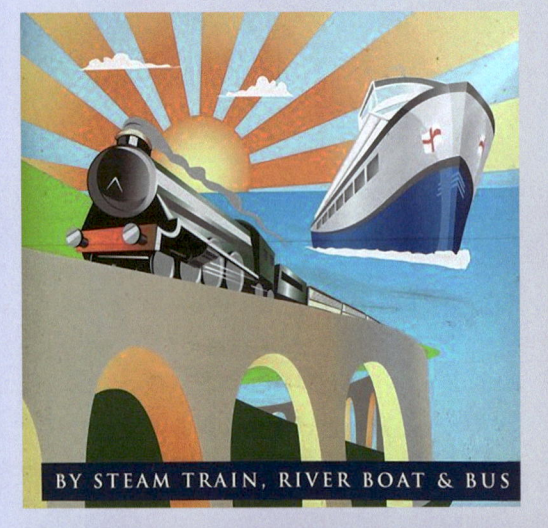

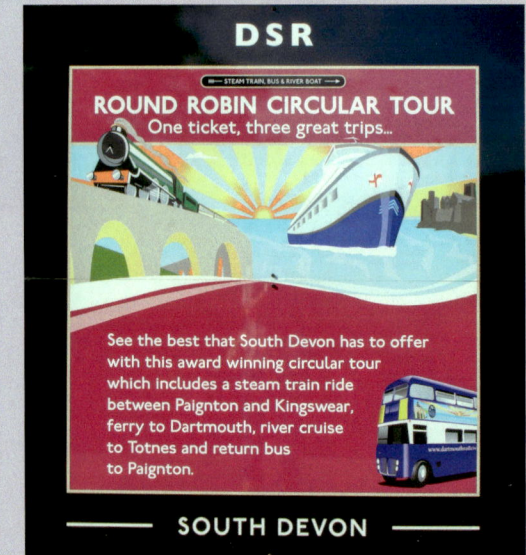

The Dartmouth Steam Railway

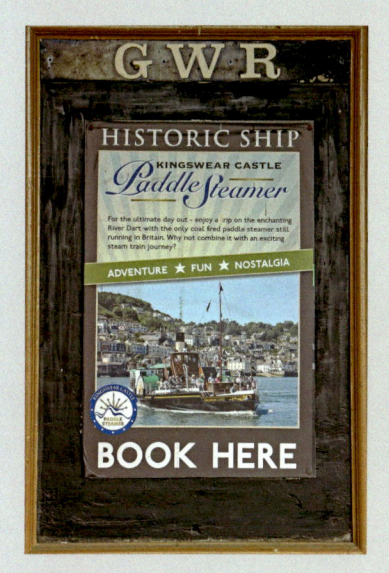

KINGSWEAR Since 2012 the paddle steamer *Kingswear Castle* has been a part of the fleet, adding a truly nostalgic element to certain cruises. *Kingswear Castle* is the last remaining coal-fired paddle steamer in operation in the UK today. She was built in 1924 at Philip & Son of Dartmouth and plied her trade between Totnes and Dartmouth until 1965. In her heyday she could carry almost 500 passengers.

The link between the railway and river steamers goes back to 1859 when Charles Seal Hayne, an investor in the early railway and steamer services, founded the Dartmouth Steam Packet Company Ltd, which was later sold to Dart Pleasure Craft – now part of the Dartmouth Steam Railway & River Boat Company.

During the Second World War the paddle steamer was used by the US Navy as a harbour tender. She was later purchased by the Paddle Steamer Preservation Society (PSPS) and left the Dart for a short spell operating from Cowes on the Isle of Wight. She then moved to Chatham in Kent where the PSPS spent 15 years fully restoring her to her former glory, after which in 1985 she commenced service offering river trips on the Medway. In 2012 she returned to her home waters of the River Dart after an absence of 47 years.

DARTMOUTH For those travellers who wish to keep their feet on terra firma, the lovely Devon town of Dartmouth is just a short ferry ride away. The town has long boasted of being the only one with a railway station but no trains! The building still stands prominent on the promenade. but is now a restaurant and take-away. When first built in 1889 the 'station' had a booking office, provided a full parcels service and even despatched motor cars down a covered gangway that ran from under the awning on the right.

The Dartmouth Steam Railway

Left: **DARTMOUTH** has many treasures to discover, including those highlighted here. The 'Boat Float', which is opposite the former station building, was an open quayside until the South Embankment was constructed in 1885. The Royal Castle Hotel was originally two prominent merchants' houses on the quayside.

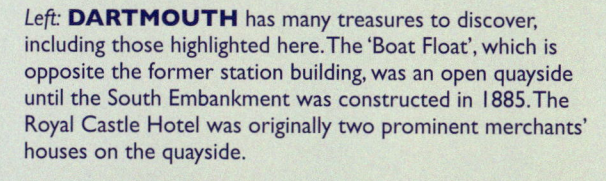

Below left: **BAYARDS COVE** Perhaps the most recognisable section of the waterfront is Bayard's Cove, which is long remembered for its association with the popular 1970s/'80s television series *The Onedin Line*. More recently it appeared in the BBC daytime drama *The Coroner*. This was originally Dartmouth's only wharf, protected by a fort at the southern end of the town.

Below: **DARTMOUTH** The 'Butterwalk' is a beautiful Tudor building that survived unchanged for 300 years before succumbing to bomb damage in 1943. Thankfully the building was restored in 1954, and now houses the town's museum.

Heading back to Paignton

Left: **HOODOWN VIADUCT** There is an autumnal tint to the trees on 3 October 2015 as *Dinmore Manor* leaves Kingswear. *Karl Heath*

Below: **HOODOWN VIADUCT** Six years earlier No 4277 *Hercules* works over the viaduct on 27 July 2009.

The Dartmouth Steam Railway

KINGSWEAR On 21 November 2015, with winter approaching, the afternoon light glints off *Hercules* and the observation coach as the train cruises along the river bank.

Inset above right: **BRITANNIA CROSSING** In this 27 July 2009 photograph the woods that form the backdrop to the line are in full leaf as *Hercules* approaches Britannia Crossing.

Above: **BRITANNIA CROSSING** The change of season is clearly evident on the trees as *Lydham Manor* heads north on 4 October 2017.

The Dartmouth Steam Railway

Below and right: **BRITANNIA CROSSING** During my October visit in 2017 I was pleased to see that the 'Manor' was working smokebox-first out of Kingswear, allowing me to get these two photographs on the Paignton side of Britannia Crossing. In the first *(below)*, on 8 October, a Kingswear departure was photographed from the road down to the Higher Ferry.

Two days earlier *(right)* an exceptionally low tide had allowed me to get down to the water's edge for this low-angle view.

DARTMOUTH Photographed over the rooftops of Dartmouth, from the road that leads up to Jawbones Hill, the last train of the day on 6 October 2017 is about to disappear into the woods as it heads back to Paignton.